Published in the United States by Bizarre Butterfly Publishing, 1347 E. San Miguel, Phoenix, Arizona 85014

ISBN: 0-915113-01-5

Library of Congress Catalog Card Number: 84-72268

Acknowledgements and permissions:
The Publicist in New York, NY, first published a few of these rules in July of 1980.

The Communicator in Phoenix, AZ, published several rules in August of 1981.

Carol Jennings of Phoenix, AZ, contributed the rule about cancelled PR projects which appears in the Science section.

Book design by Pat Kenny
Cartoons by Rick Kirkman

Roger's Rules of Public Relations

By William Roger Davis
and
Judy Green Davis

Table of Contents

Introduction

I don't really remember the first rule that Judy and I wrote. Perhaps it was in some meaningless meeting when one of us wrote a summary of the silliness of it all.

Or maybe it was after one of us had been chewed out by a client for something that was not our fault.

Or one time when we couldn't get anyone to use a story that a client wanted in the papers.

Or when we were trying to explain to our friends what we do in public relations.

Ultimately, the list of our rules grew into a book, stimulated by the situations that face communications practitioners day after day. The rules became our response to the thrills and pain of our careers. So, although this is far from a serious book, it is thoughtfully presented to all communications professionals with empathy for the stress of their work.

We have not knowingly collected a rule from another source, except in one instance which is acknowledged in the front of this book. We wrote all the rest on matchbooks, business cards, table napkins, scraps of paper, and whatever was handy. We wrote them at home, at work, in Europe, in transit and interminably.

The task consumed us to the point that we had to finish it so that we could get some sleep and get on to other projects.

Now it is done, and in book form. At last we can forget about writing rules of public relations. And that suggests a rule:

Writing the rules of public relations is always better than being the rulee.

Roger Davis
Phoenix, Arizona
1984

Public Relations Science

*The elements of good writing are:
clarity, accuracy, brevity,
stapling, folding, sorting, and stuffing.*

A random sample, no matter how selected, always includes a disproportionate share of your adversaries and two people who are currently suing you.

A PR program always can be evaluated by counting the newspaper clippings; unless there aren't any, in which case you must apply truly professional techniques.

A survey that shows good results
is never questioned.
A bad survey is
examined and reexamined
while the credentials
of the surveyor
are called into question.

Carol Jennings' rule of
budgetary balances:
The more work
a PR project entails,
the more likely it is
to be cancelled
halfway to completion.

The simpler the message,
the greater the misunderstanding.

A failure to communicate
always is followed
by over-tell.

The PR profession always
is the last to recognize the need
for communicating about itself.

Preventive PR always is
practiced next time.

The elements of good writing are:
clarity, accuracy, brevity, stapling,
folding, sorting and stuffing.

If Murphy had engaged
professional PR counsel,
you would know Murphy's
first name.

PR is the social conscience
of an organization–if
the organization
is run by humans.

PR is the delicate art
of satisfying the annoyed
while not annoying
the satisfied.

A speech about PR
at an out-of-town convention
always sounds more profound
than it really is.

Public relations always seems
to improve everyone's image
except its own.

Public Relations People

Explaining what public relations is usually results in the response, "Yes, but what do you do?"

PR people are the last to know
and the last to admit it.

Most people believe that PR people
have lots of free time
and are good listeners.

As an issue becomes more complex
and splintered, a PR person always
considers the possibility of
becoming a freelance writer.

The world's best PR person
is totally unknown.

When people see a public relations
person reading the newspaper, they
assume he/she is having fun.

Explaining what public relations
is usually results in the response,
"Yes, but what do you do?"

People who "like people" always
make poor PR practitioners.

When public relations
people dream, they dream
in column inches.

Putting "30" at the end of a news
release makes you think that you
can write.

When serving on the board
of a charitable organization,
you always are made the chair
of the PR committee.

When you paraphrase a nice set of words from your research, it will turn out that the original author lives in your hometown and will charge plagarism.

Attorneys are entering the PR field in growing numbers.
The court of public opinion will listen to anyone, even amateur public relations practitioners.

Any statement which begins,
"PR is your field, not mine," will
result in advice that you can't use.
        But you'll never be able
        to make the advisor
        understand why.

The best speech writer always
sounds terrible on his/her feet.

Whenever two PR people
are in a place together,
the subject always will turn to:
"Is PR a science or an art?"
	And the discussion will
	conclude with an exploration
	of how the profession
	is misunderstood.

A PR person who
self-publishes a book
has a fool for a publisher.

The Media

Major disasters usually happen on days scheduled for press events.

There never will come a time when the word "flack" will disappear from the lexicon of journalists.

A degree in PR never is a good substitute for six months as a starving reporter.

The chances of a news release being used are inversely proportional to the number of people at the newspaper who remember you used to work there for peanuts and "sold out" for the "big time."

The evolution of PR started when a
public relations person stood erect
and issued a three-page news
release on it.

The media never calls on a quiet
day unless you've left the office.

A short, critical, inaccurate letter
to the editor is always perceived as
having more impact on public
opinion than a lengthy, good
story on page two.

Off the record never is.

A solid tip that grows into a good
story will endear the PR person to
an editor forever
        or until the next issue,
        whichever comes first.

The more complex the issue,
the younger the reporter
sent to cover it.

The messier the situation,
the slower the news day.

Major disasters usually happen on
days with scheduled press events.

"No comment" always results
in at least two paragraphs
of negative copy on page one.

Reporters whose beats include very
complex and important issues
know their articles are generally
not read by the public.
No one at the paper
reads them either.

The evolution of P.R. started when a public relations person
stood erect and issued a
three-page news release on it.

The fewer the facts,
the better the story.

A television public service
announcement that you produced
always is run after you've
gone to bed.

The first thing you learn in an
introduction to journalism course
is that PR pays more money and is,
therefore, an inferior profession.

Corporate
Public
Relations

The best PR campaign in the world
will fail if you don't get coverage
in the CEO's favorite magazine.

Public relations should function
at the decision-making level
of the corporation, assuming that
there is one.

The less important the topic,
the more coverage the CEO
will demand.

Whenever there is a severe cut in
the corporate budget and therefore
a real need to communicate,
the public relations budget will be
sacrificed first.

When management has a problem,
they call for public relations.
When they don't have a problem,
they call for everyone else.
As a result, public relations
people always are in the middle
when there's trouble; on the
outside when something good
happens; and on the inside
when it's not important.

One critical letter will get
more attention than it deserves,
while one letter of praise
never gets enough.

If the first public relations person
had come from the ranks of
pots-and-pans salespeople, every
employer would demand that you
have at least some experience of
this kind.

The best PR campaign in the world
will fail if you don't get coverage in
the CEO's favorite magazine.

The only typo in the new brochure
always will be discovered
by the CEO.

The CEO's secretary
is the PR person's best friend.

A name-selection contest among
employees always results in an
unwieldy, semi-literate
winning selection.
        Management will never be able
to expunge the name.

If management won't buy it —
add some more three and four
syllable words and a two-color
flow chart.

If employees believe that the CEO
writes his/her own speeches,
the CEO will begin to believe
that the expressed ideas are
his/her own.
        The CEO will later come to
        believe that he/she doesn't
        need a speechwriter at all.

In the approval cycle for an article,
the first level of management will
add a fact, the second level will edit
that fact, and the third level
will remove it.

The top PR officer in any company
is the CEO's spouse's best friend.

An employee who complains
about your new logo is not paying
attention to his or her own job.

No matter which photo you
choose to use, it will be of the
CEO's bad side.
        The CEO's spouse
        will like the photo.

In corporate communications,
every member of the corporation
has two jobs – his/her own
and that of the employee
communications editor.

Take an out-of-town assignment
and everyone will conclude you went for the
late nights, expense account dinners and booze...
no matter how well you handle the work.

When an organization wants to
disguise the fact that it has a
public relations department,
someone will suggest calling it
"issues management."

The phrase "What we need is some
PR" is usually followed by one of
three courses of action:
     – resignation of the CEO;
     – propaganda and coverups; or
     – none.

When a corporate manager asks
the public relations officer to
"PR the copy more," the manager
really means "add some puff to
make it longer and more palatable."

The need for more people to get
out a big job will occur on Friday at
5:35 p.m.

PR professionals must continue to
educate management about the
importance of public relations or
management will begin to think
that the PR staff doesn't know that
management exists.

Take an out-of-town assignment
and everyone will conclude you
went for the late nights,
expense account dinners
and booze . . . no matter
how well you handle the work.

The only story impossible to write
is one about your own promotion.

Corporations are always
filled with "no-men" when
approvals are sought for
communications programs.

Publications

Most major revisions to the annual report will be made on the blueline.

After you get another job
and stop editing a publication,
it will go downhill.

The more needed a publication is,
the more likely it is to be
eliminated by management.

The more people working on a
publication, the worse it will read.

No PR person truly believes
that the average person
spends less than 10 minutes
reading the annual report.

No matter how carefully
the annual report is proofed,
a typo will slip through,
and it will be in the name
of a company executive.

The less money the editor spends
producing the annual report,
the less credibility he/she
will have.
On the other hand,
he/she will probably have to
produce it only once.

Most major revisions to the
annual report will be made
on the blueline.

The CEO will read every word
in company publications on a
regular basis.
The head of the
PR department will read
those same publications
only occasionally . . .
or when someone complains
about a story.

Issues
and Publics

Dealing with the climate of public opinion is like predicting the weather.

"Issues Management"
was dreamed up by a thoughtful
public relations person who wanted
a raise.

As soon as you fulfill an
expectation of society,
there will be a change
in society's expectation.

Appealing to another person's
self-interest always results
in a charge that you forced
someone to do something
they had no interest in doing.

You can make a sow's ear
look like a silk purse,
      but the public eventually
      will smell it anyway.

A public relations program
that has a low profile
will produce a high profile
for an organization's
worst problems.

Dealing with the climate
of public opinion is like
predicting the weather.

The conflicting forces of society are
public relations' bread and board.

A socially responsive act always
results in an accusation that you
did it for some devious purpose.

Your critics often will cry
for facts based on their own
emotional arguments.

The most critical public issues
always bore the public.

Your most irrational critic
will get the most coverage.
The coverage will make the
irrational critic look wise and
remarkably far-sighted.

- The more explanations you issue,
the more confused the subject
will get.

- Public skepticism
follows everything.

Editors

Roger's Law of Existence:
I edit; therefore, I am.

Never write negative copy.

A good editor with a sharp red
pencil can make even the best story
look like flag day at Red Square.

A good definition of public
relations always needs editing.

For every great headline
that has a negative in it,
there's always one person
who says negatives don't sell.

A good editor does.

Agencies and Consultants

If you bid high because the client is a buffoon
you'd rather not work for,
you'll get the account.

The client is always right,
except when you lose the account.

Once a reporter becomes
knowledgeable about your
client's issues, the reporter will
leave town.
Or the reporter will steal your
client and open a new agency.

An advertising "make good"
always will contain an error.

If you buy a reporter three
martinis for lunch, later you'll
think that you could have sold the
story if you had bought four.

If Shakespeare had been a
public relations man, he would
have been an unknown writer
because his freelance stuff
obviously had a hidden sell
for one of his clients.

Public relations often is
confused with advertising.
Or is it advertising that is confused
with public relations?

Any order of advertising
specialties for gifts guaranteed
for two weeks delivery will
arrive one week late.

The more personable and
intelligent the new agency head is,
the sooner he or she is liable to be
transferred to the agency branch in
Tuscaloosa.
Agency heads that remain for
years never know how
to throw fun parties.

When an agency issues an announcement that it is expanding into new, more modern office space in a better location, it probably means:

    A. They lost their trade-out account
    B. They found a better trade-out account
    C. Their lease was voided for a slow payment
    D. They're moving closer to home to save gas and lunch expenses
    E. They're doing well and expanding

Frequent notices in the ad club
bulletin about client acquisitions
for a new agency mean the new
agency is not making money.

The smaller the account,
the more changes
the client will make
in the copy.

If you bid high because the client is
a buffoon you'd rather not work for,
you'll get the account.
If you bid low because the
account looks exciting, you'll
lose out to a higher priced
agency.

• The bigger the job,
the slower the client will pay.

Agency people serving on
community boards are always asked
to design a new logo for free.
　　As soon as work is underway
　　on the new logo, the agency
　　representative will resign from
　　the agency to open a cute cafe.

Graphic Arts

Special paper ordered from the mill
always disappears somewhere near Oshkosh.

A photo spread of a company
social function which appears in
the house organ always will feature
at least one person with
someone else's spouse.

On any given contact sheet,
the photograph with the best image
of the CEO will have
at least one person with a post
growing out of his/her head.

The staff photographer is
always on vacation.

One photo of the CEO's spouse
in the company publication is
equivalent to 10 inches of copy
about the CEO.

In the only useable photo,
there always will be at least one
person in the center
that no one can identify.

The simpler the idea, the longer
the artist will take to develop it.

The section of clip art that you need to fill a critical hole in your publication will be missing on your deadline day.

The art department always is swamped with rush jobs.
    Half of those jobs are at the CEO's express demand.

No matter what service you request, the art department says it used to offer that service until the budget was cut.

If the regular eight-page issue
of your publication takes a day
to paste-up, a one-page special issue
also will take a full day to paste-up.

The more lead time there is for a
project, the shorter the time the
print shop will be given.

When the print shop turns
the job around unusually fast,
there always is an irreparable
error of fact in the copy.
Four copies of the bad issue will
leak out. One will go to the
union business manager and at
least one will go to the
company CEO.

Special paper ordered from the mill
always disappears somewhere
near Oshkosh.

The low bidder always delivers
a week late.
The high bidder does on-time
work for your competition.

Artist fees are proportionate to the
prior information they have about
how much is budgeted.
An artist always states the fee
after saying, "It depends . . ."

A rush job never is.

Machinery only breaks down
on deadline days.

Special Events

At a meeting for:
- more than 200 people, one slide will will be upside down;
- more than 300 people, one slide will have a spelling error;
- more than 700, there will be microphone feedback; and
- more than 1,000, the sound system will fail entirely.

A carefully prepared list of potential questions and answers for a news event question and answer session will result in no questions being asked.

Management role-playing for the question and answer session will result in no media showing up at all.

Any public relations event involving more than 5,000 people always results in at least four lawsuits.

An up-to-date mailing list will include at least three people who died 15 years ago.

Closing rule:

For every good rule in this book,
there's someone out there
who has a topper.

You probably have some rules laughing around in your head or stuck on an office bulletin board. Send those rules to us. We'd like to use them in a future book or article. Please let us know the exact source for the quote so that we can give proper credit.

Roger and Judy
c/o Bizarre Butterfly Publishing
1347 E. San Miguel
Phoenix, AZ 85014

William Roger Davis holds a degree in radio and television. He has worked as an editor of a small town newspaper, a television cameraman, an advertising agency account executive, and a corporate public relations executive. Presently, Roger is involved in issues management, whatever that is.

Judy Green Davis has worked in many facets of corporate public relations in three major industries: finance, utilities, and electronics/high tech. She currently owns a public relations agency in Phoenix, Arizona. Judy holds a degree in cultural anthropology, which always gets a laugh on her resumé.

Colophon:

This volume is the third book published
by Bizarre Butterfly Publishing. The text type is
Goudy Oldstyle, set in 20 point on a Mergenthaler
with a Penta system. Text paper is Mountie Matt
70 pound.

This edition consists of one thousand copies.